10,000 MANIACS

ANTHOLOGY

AMSCO PUBLICATIONS
NEW YORK • LONDON • SYDNEY

Natalie Merchant

Robert Buck

Dennis Drew

ANTHOLOGY

10,000 MANIACS

Steven Gustafson

Jerome Augustyniak

Cover and inside spread design by Natalie Merchant
Photography by Betty Cheung
Music arrangements by Frank Metis

Copyright © 1993 by Christian Burial Music
This book published 1993 by Amsco Publications,
A Division of Music Sales Corporation, New York, NY.

Order No. AM 91243
International Standard Book Number: 0.8256.1359.0

Exclusive Distributors:
Music Sales Corporation
225 Park Avenue South, New York, NY 10003 USA

Printed in the United States of America by
Vicks Lithograph and Printing Corporation

CAN'T IGNORE THE TRAIN

Music: John Lombardo
Lyric: Natalie Merchant

Through ad - ven - ture, we are ___ not ad - ven - ture -

EVERYONE A PUZZLE LOVER

Music: John Lombardo
Lyric: Natalie Merchant

gild - ed plaques,___ grace their stud - y walls,___

cor - dion pleats___ *(See additional lyrics)*

___ hide the cracks,___ While their gen - i - us___ is turned___ to

works of tyr - an - ny.___ Then off to mar - ket, to

mar - ket go,___ sell - ing these.___

where they go, ____ dis - dain and jeer - ing

for fools to call ___ the no - ble peas - an - try. ___

Oh, how it puz - zles me.

To Coda ⊕

D.S. to 2nd ending
al Coda 𝄉

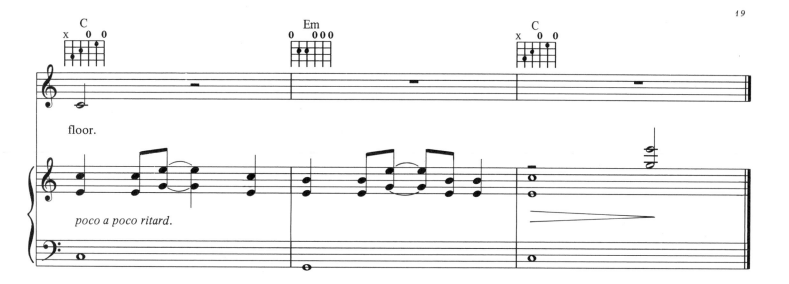

floor.

poco a poco ritard.

Additional lyrics

2. And why are some men born
   With a fate of poverty?
   One firm bed for a swollen back,
   Year by year the bodies wracked,
   While their obedience is had with gradual defeat
   By the pace, by the pace and the urgency.

   Through a muddled thought they phrase it,
   God knows we're deceived...
   (To 2nd ending)

3. I pressed flat the accordion pleats
   That had gathered in his cotton sleeves,
   While he thumbed, yes, thumbed –
   I wouldn't say caressed –
   The final piece, a mountain's crest,
   Soon to reply assuredly.

   Oh, for man aged ninety years,
   No words to waste on sermons, he'd be
   (To 2nd ending)
   Pleased to answer short or sincere. *(To Bridge)*

   Girl, there's nonsense
   In all these heaven measures.
   It's a heathen creed,
   So your grandma says,
   But better to live by...
   Drink it all before it's dry.
   (3-bar instrumental to Coda ⊕)

BACK O' THE MOON

Music: Dennis Drew
Lyric: Natalie Merchant

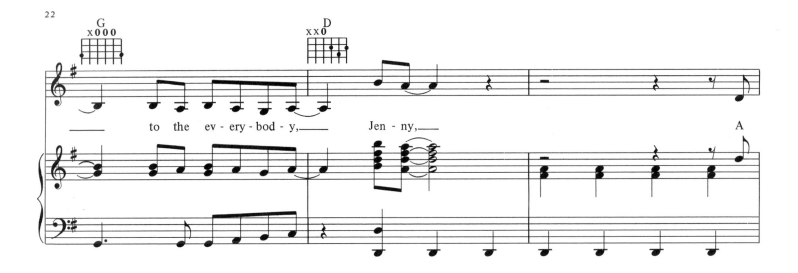

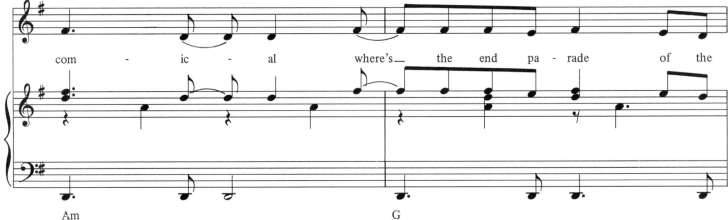

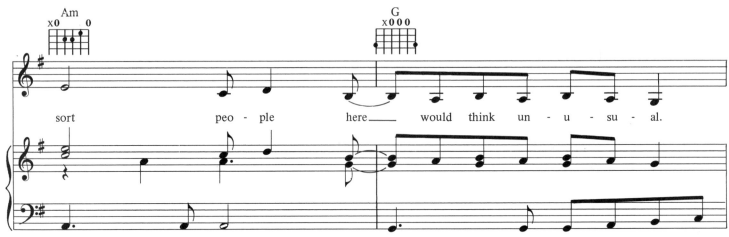

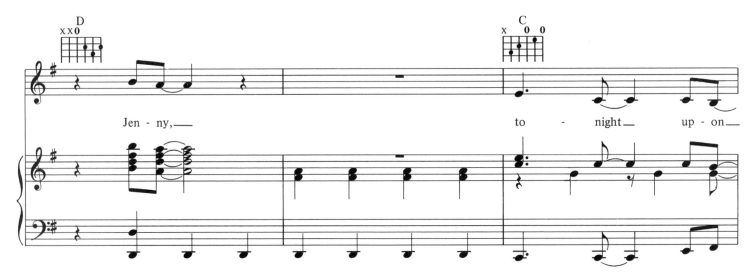

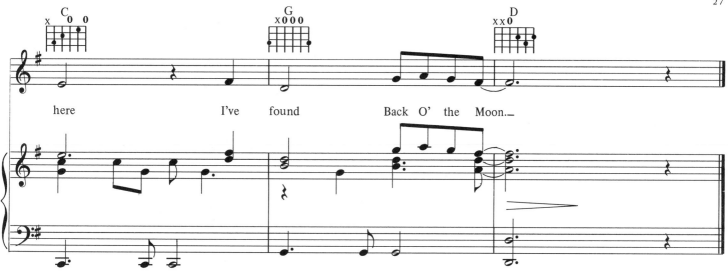

here   I've   found   Back O' the Moon.__

Additional lyrics

2. Jenny,
   Jenny, you don't know the days I tried
   Telling backyard tales
   So to maybe amuse.
   Oh, your mood is never giddy,
   If you smile, I'm delighted,
   But you'd rather pout.
   Such a lazy child,
   You dare fold your arms,
   Tisk and say that I lie.

   There's one rare and odd style of thinking,
   Part only known to the everybody, Jenny.
   The small step and giant leap takers
   Got the head start in the racing toward it.

   Jenny,
   Tonight upon the mock brine of a Luna Sea,
   Far off we sail on...
   (To 2nd ending & bridge)

3. Jenny,
   Jenny, you don't know the nights I hide
   Below a second storey room,
   To whistle you down.
   Oh, the man who's let to divvy up
   Time is a miser,
   He's got a silver coin,
   Lets it shine for hours
   While you sleep it away.
   There's one...
   (To Coda ⊕)

AMONG THE AMERICANS

Music: Robert Buck, Dennis Drew
Lyric: Natalie Merchant

Dance to the sun,—

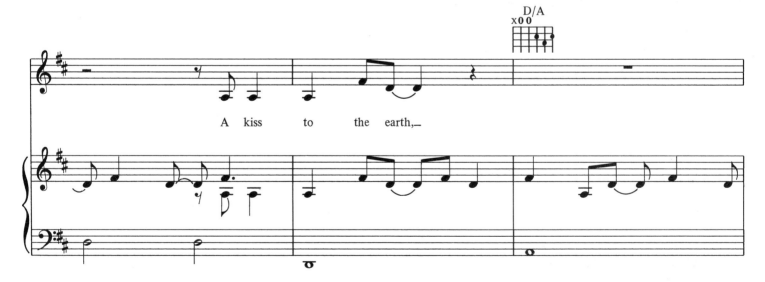

A kiss to the earth,—

*Cherokee name for Andrew Jackson, the 7th president of the U.S.A.

pale and died

by your god's de - cree,

For he ha - ted

me.

A CAMPFIRE SONG

Words and Music by Natalie Merchant

1. A lie to say, "Oh, my mountain has coal veins and beds to dig. Five hundred men with axes and they all dig for me."

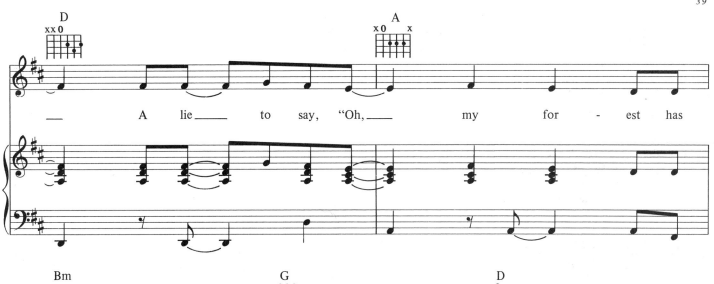

A lie___ to say, "Oh,___ my for-est has

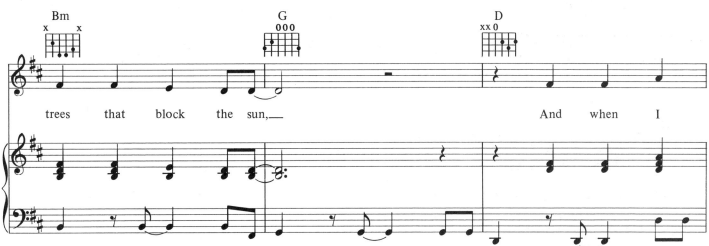

trees that block the sun,___ And when I

cut them down, I don't ans-wer to an-y-

one." No, no, no, nev-er will he be-lieve that his

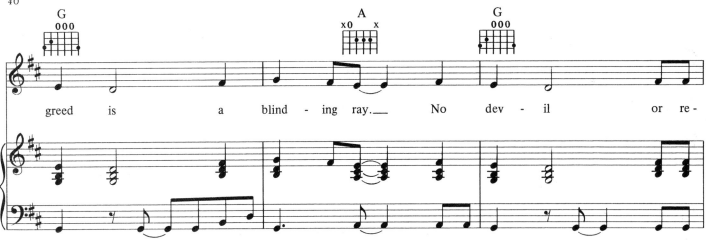

greed is a blind - ing ray.___ No dev - il or re-

deem - er can cheat him. He'll

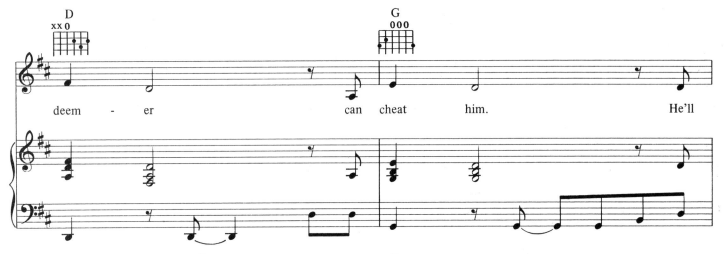

take his gold ___ where he's ly - ing cold. ___

___ La la la la la la ___ la, La la la

la la la. _____ La la la la la la la la,

La la la la la la la, Lone - ly, lone - ly,

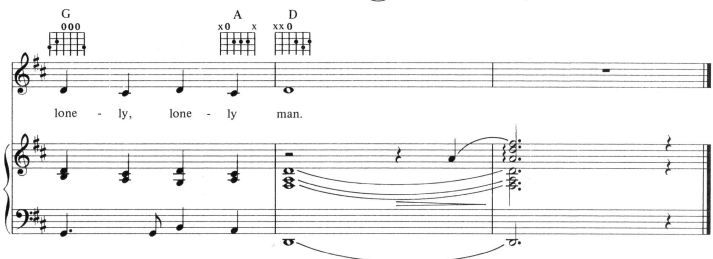

lone - ly, lone - ly man.

Additional Lyrics

2. A lie to say, "Oh my, mine gave a diamond big as a fist."
   But with every gem is his pocket, the jewels he has missed.

   A lie to say, "Oh, my garden is growing taller by the day."
   He only eats the best and tosses the rest away.

   Oh no, never will he believe that his greed is a blinding ray.
   No devil or redeemer can cheat him.
   He'll take his gold to where he's lying cold,

   (to 2nd ending: Six deep in the grave*).*

WHAT'S THE MATTER HERE?

Words and Music by Robert Buck and Natalie Merchant

LIKE THE WEATHER

Words and Music by Natalie Merchant

Moderately, with a moving beat

and so I breathe. Late - ly it___ seems this___

___ big bed___ is where___ I nev - er leave.

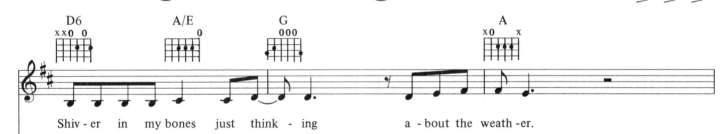

Shiv - er in my bones just think - ing a - bout the weath - er.

A quiv - er in my voice___ as I cry:___

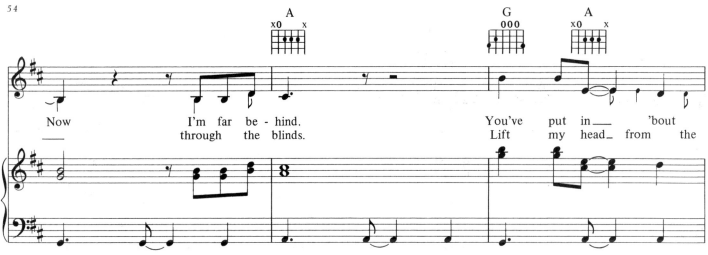

Now   I'm far be - hind.   You've put in ___ 'bout
through the blinds.   Lift   my head_ from the

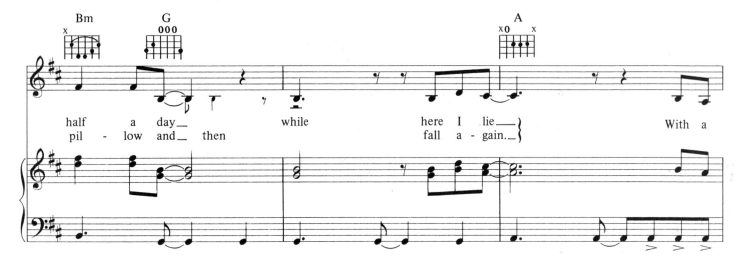

half   a day___   while   here I lie___
pil - low and_ then   fall a - gain.___   With a

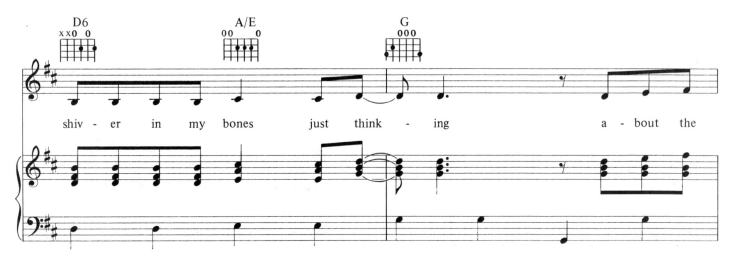

shiv - er in my bones   just think - ing   a - bout the

weath - er.   A quiv - er in my___ voice

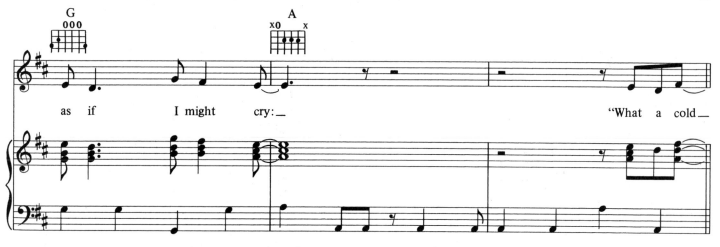

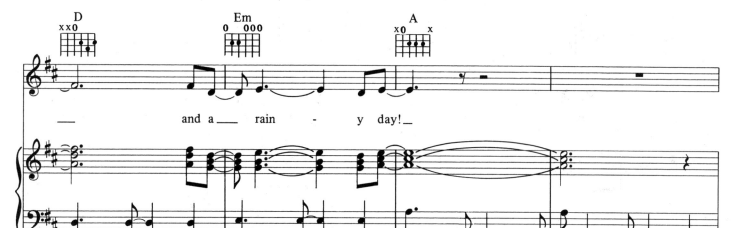

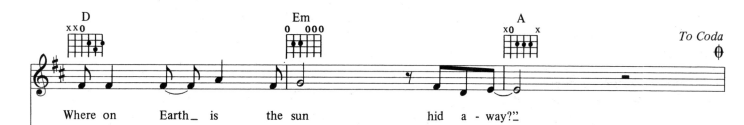

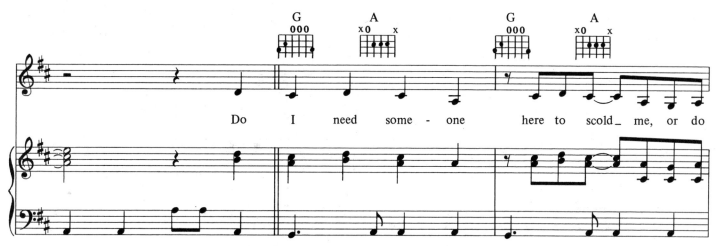

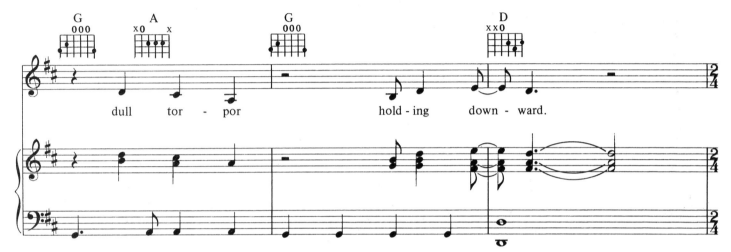

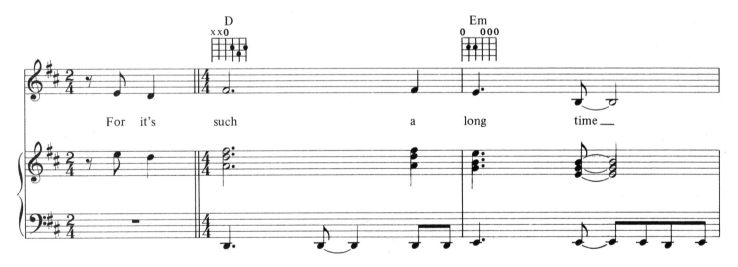

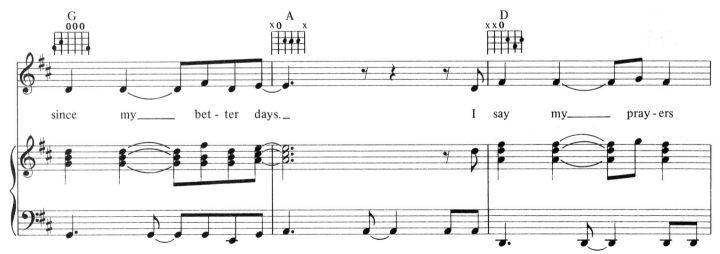

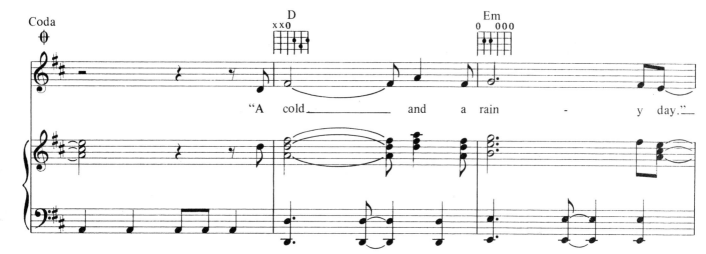

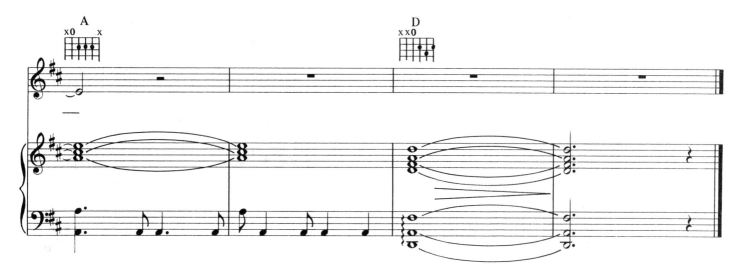

DON'T TALK

Words and Music by Dennis Drew and Natalie Merchant

Moderately, with a steady beat

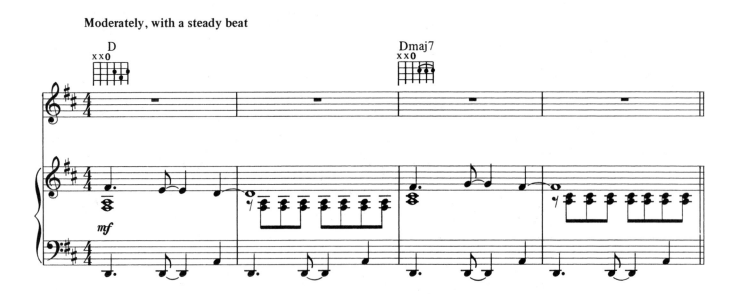

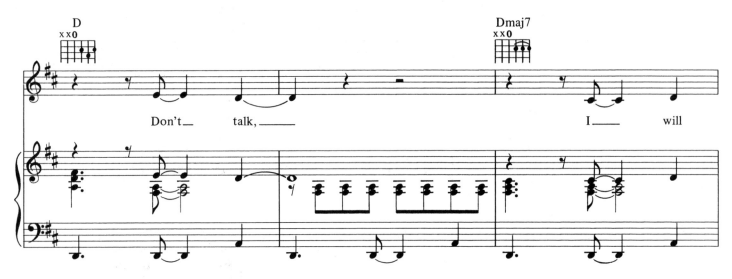

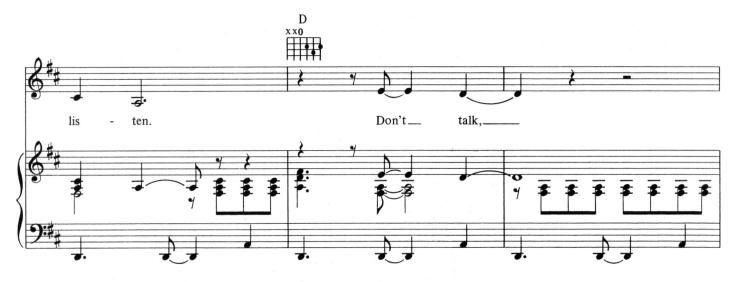

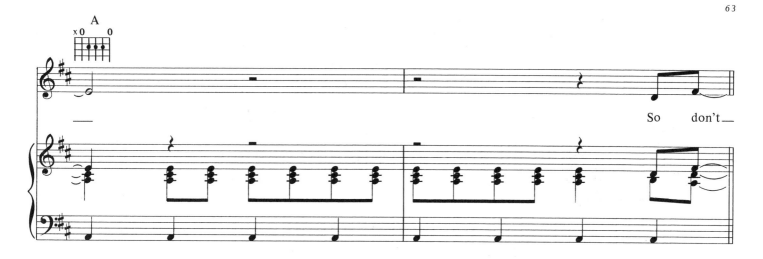

So don't

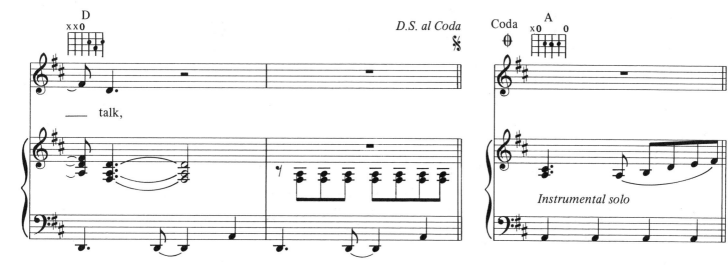

talk,

D.S. al Coda

Coda

Instrumental solo

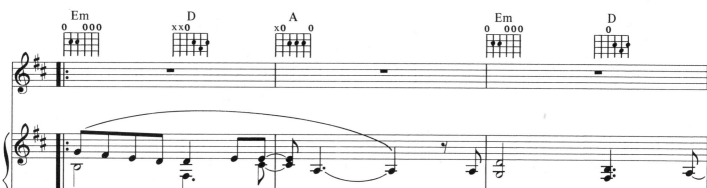

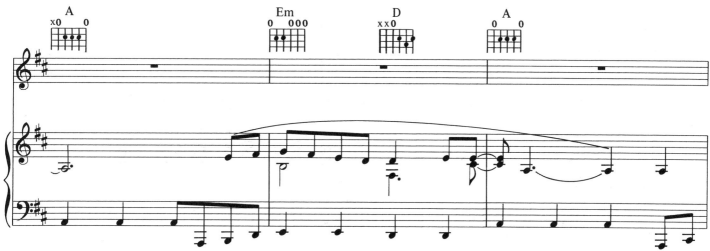

𝄋 (So don't talk), I was sleeping.
Don't talk, let me go on dreaming.
How your eyes they glow so fiercely,
I can tell that you're inspired
By the name you just chose for me.
Now what was it?
Oh, never mind it.

We will talk, talk, talk about this
When your head is clear.
I'll discuss this in the morning,
But until then
You may talk but I won't hear. *(to Coda)*

VERDI CRIES

Words and Music by Natalie Merchant

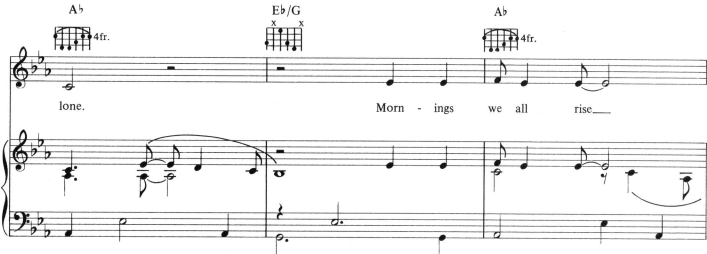

I ___ fill the bath and climb ___ in - side   sing - ing.

poco rit.

La, ___ la, la,   la, la, la.

a tempo

La, ___ la, la,   la, la, la.

He will ___ not touch the pas - try, but ev - ery day they bring him

THE BIG PARADE

Music: Jerome Augustyniak
Words: Natalie Merchant

Additional Lyrics

𝄋 4. Near a soldier, an ex-Marine
    With a tattooed dagger and an eagle trembling.
    He bites his lip beside a widow breaking down.
    She takes her Purple Heart, makes a fist, strikes The Wall.

    All come to live a dream,
    To join the slowest parade they'll ever see.
    Their weight of sorrows carried far,
    All taken to The Wall.

    It's ... *(To Coda)*

DUST BOWL

Music: Robert Buck
Words: Natalie Merchant

Flowingly

know   to leave them home.   They fol - low

me through the store with these toys   I can't af - ford.   "Kids,—

take them back,__ you know__ bet-ter than that." Dolls that

talk, as-tro-nauts, T. V. games, air-planes,__ they don't un-der-stand,__ and

how can I__ ex - plain? I try and try, but I can't

save.__ Pen-nies, nick-els,

and the last let-ters in three of their names.__

This__ lot-ter-y's__ been build-ing up for weeks.__

__ I could be luck-y me with the five mil-lion prize, tears of

dis-be-lief__ spill-ing out of my eyes.__ I try and

D.S. al Fine

TROUBLE ME

Music: Dennis Drew
Words: Natalie Merchant

Moderately, with a beat

Trou - ble...

1. Trou-ble me, dis - turb me with
2. Speak to me, why are you build-ing with this

all your cares and your wor - ries. Trou - ble me
thick brick wall to de - fend me. Speak to me

EAT FOR TWO

Music and Words: Natalie Merchant

Dream child in my head __ is a night-mare born in a bor-rowed bed. __ Now I know light-ning strikes a-gain. __

__ It struck me once, __

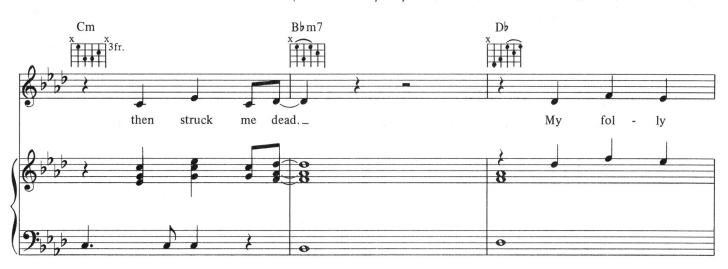

then struck me dead. __ My fol-ly

94

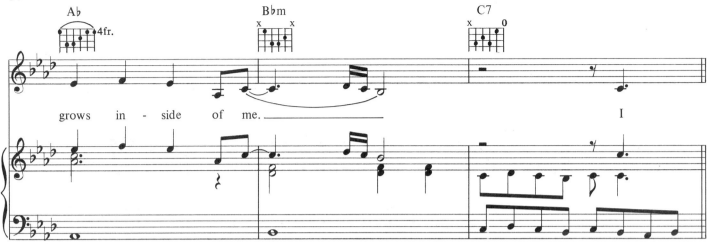

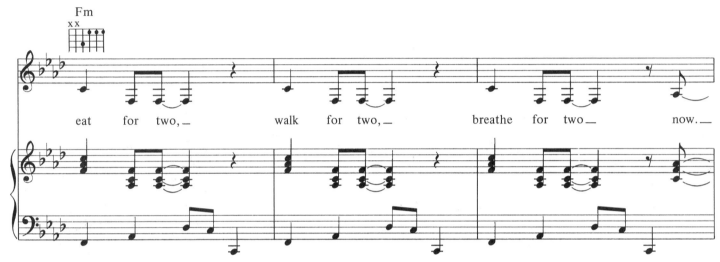

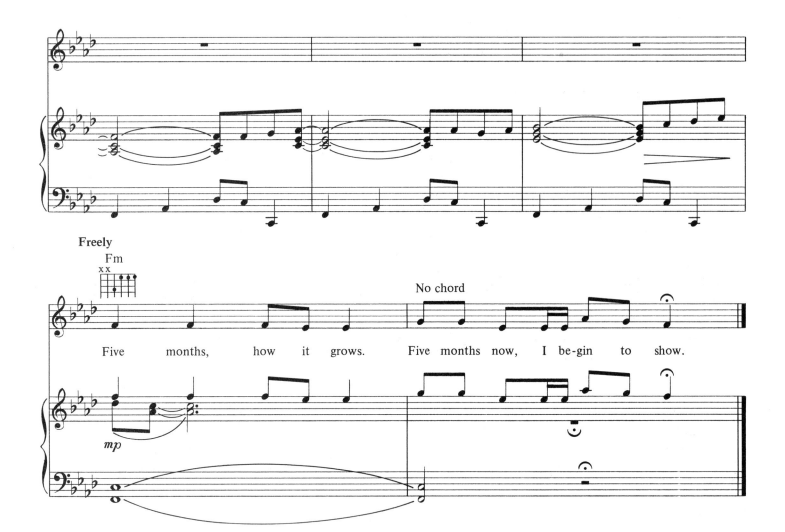

Freely

Fm

No chord

Five months, how it grows. Five months now, I be-gin to show.

mp

Additional Lyrics

2. Well, the egg man fell down off his shelf.
   All the good king's men with all their help
   Struggled 'til the end
   For a shell they couldn't mend.

   You know where this will lead,
   To hush and rock in the nursery
   For the kicking one
   Inside of me.

   I eat for two, walk for two, breathe for two now.
   Eat for two, walk for two, breathe for two now.

3. When the boy was a boy, and a girl was a girl,
   And they found each other in a wicked world.
   Strong in some respects,
   But she couldn't stand for the way he begged

   And gave in. Pride is for men.
   Young girls should run and hide instead.
   Risk the game
   By taking dares with "yes."

   Eat for two, walk for two, breathe for two now.
   Eat for two, walk for two, breathe for two now. *(To 3rd ending)*

THESE ARE DAYS

Buck/Merchant

Moderately, with a steady beat

Capo on 1st fret:

These are days you'll re- mem-ber.

1. Nev-er be-fore and nev-er since,
2. When May is rush-ing o-ver you

I prom-ise, with de-sire

will the whole

you with de-sire to be part of the

THE LATIN ONE

Lombardo/Owen

help - less sight he plung - es at me,— chok - ing, gut - ter - ing,

drown - ing. Put in a wag - on, he—

had to keep pace,— as— his— eyes melt in his face.

Instrumental solo

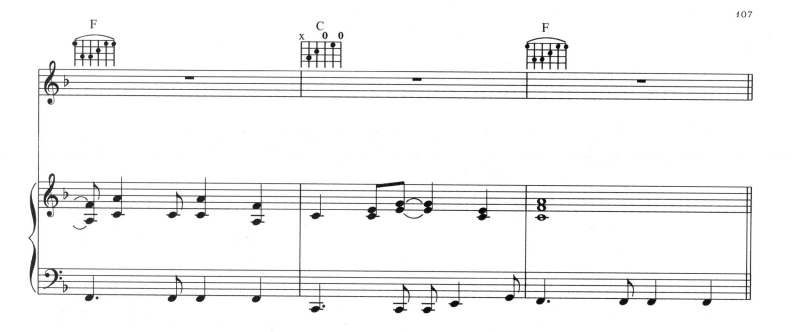

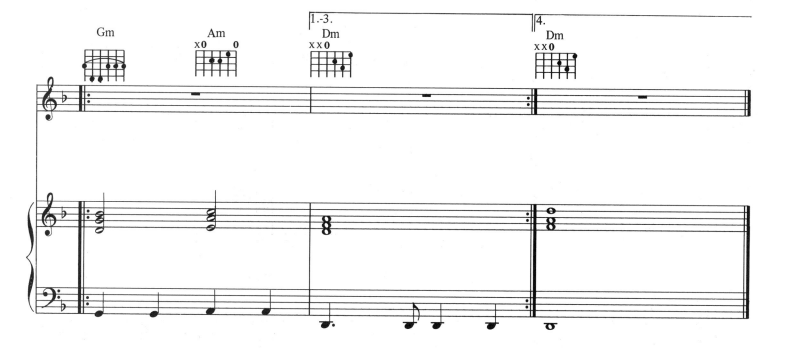

Additional lyrics

3. If you could hear blood
   Gurgling from ruptured lungs,
   If you could witness
   Vile sores on innocent tongues,
   You would not tell me,
   Not with such pride and such zest,
   The lies of history:
   Dulce et decorum est
   Pro patria mori.
   Some desperate glory,
   Pro patria mori,
   As witness disturbs the story.
   (To Coda ⊕)

107

KATRINA'S FAIR

Buck/Merchant

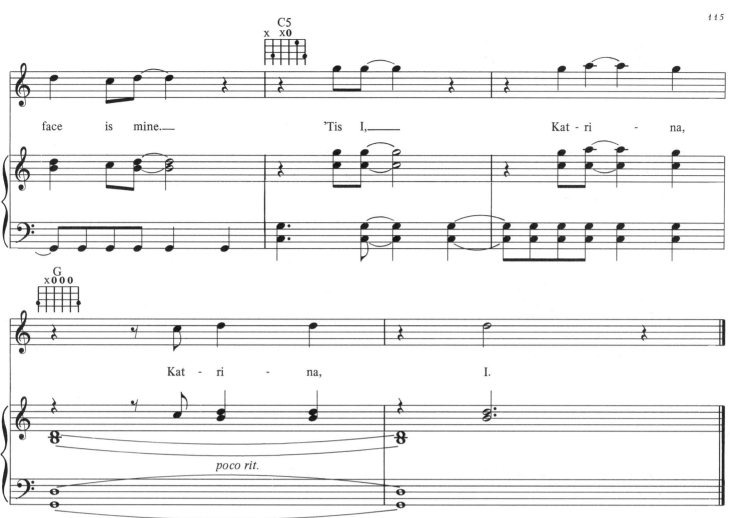

Additional lyrics

2. Marguerite, vigilant,
She dwells on frigid casements.
And Sarah's thoughts in high velocity,
Accusations always pierce and pass.
Clara abandons her passions for distastes.
And Miss Lenora P. Sinclair
Early for coffee in the pool,
"I'm resituating all your words."
Capital, space, colon, and paragraph.

But it's Katrina's fair Tuesday morning,
As she with caution unlatches the flat door.
She alone cascades to the basement,
Carefully not to spoil her
Calico printed pinafore composite traits and mannerists.
(To 2nd ending)

STOCKTON GALA DAYS

Buck/Drew/Gustafson/Augustyniak/Merchant

But you'll nev - er, you'll __ nev - er

know. How I've

poco rit.

JEZEBEL

Merchant

Moderate, somewhat freely

1. To think of my task is chil - ling. To know I was
2. *(See additional lyrics)*

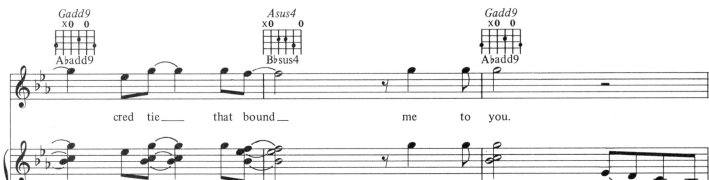

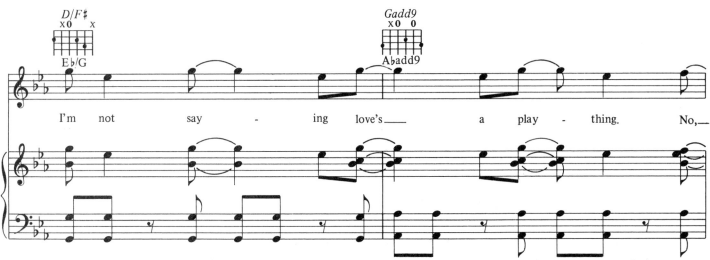

blind - fold __ o - ver both our eyes.

Additional Lyrics

2. You lie there, an innocent baby.
   I feel like the thief who is raiding your home,
   Entering and breaking and taking in every room.
   I know your feelings are tender
   And that inside you the embers still glow.
   But I'm a shadow,
   I'm only a bed of blackened coal.
   Call myself Jezebel for wanting to leave.